Jefferson County
R.J. Bailar Public Library
OCT 19 2020
375 South Water Street
Monticello, FL 32344
(850) 342-0205

12 WOMEN IN MEDIA

by Brianna L. DeVore

www.12StoryLibrary.com

Copyright © 2020 by 12-Story Library, Mankato, MN 56002. All rights reserved. No part of this book may be reproduced or utilized in any form or by any means without written permission from the publisher.

12-Story Library is an imprint of Bookstaves.

Photographs ©: Amanpourtátk/CC4.0, cover, 1; PBS NewsHour/CC2.0, 4; Don Emmert/Associated Press, 5; Neil Grabowsky/Montclair Film/CC2.0, 6; Ron Adar/Shutterstock.com, 7; John Mathew Smith & www.celebrity-photos.com/CC2.0, 8; Pete Souza/PD, 9; Anefo/PD, 10; Associated Press, 11; PD, 11; Ovidiu Hrubaru/Shutterstock.com, 12; PippiLongstocking/Shutterstock.com, 12; Debby Wong/Shutterstock.com, 13; JStone/Shutterstock.com, 14; Jason Lee/Associated Press, 15; Ossewa/CC3.0, 15; Lou Rocco/ABC/Walt Disney Television/CC2.0, 16; Kathy Hutchins/Shutterstock.com, 16; Bret Hartman/TED/CC2.0, 17; Kathy Hutchins/Shutterstock.com, 18; Barry King/Alamy, 19; PD, 19; Kristy Walker/Fortune Conferences/CC2.0, 20; PD, 21; Glenn Dettwiler/CC2.0, 22; PD, 23; Angel Manzano/Getty Images, 24; Piotr Swat/Shutterstock.com, 25; Hadrian/Shutterstock.com, 25; Amanpourtátk/CC4.0, 26; atomtetsuwan2002/CC2.0, 27; Judith Sedwick/Schlesinger Library/PD, 28; PD, 29

ISBN
9781632357786 (hardcover)
9781632358875 (paperback)
9781645820581 (ebook)

Library of Congress Control Number: 2019938621

Printed in the United States of America
September 2019

About the Cover
Christiane Amanpour in 2015.

Access free, up-to-date content on this topic plus a full digital version of this book. Scan the QR code on page 31 or use your school's login at 12StoryLibrary.com.

Table of Contents

Gwen Ifill: Television Pioneer 4

Samantha Bee: Commenting with Comedy 6

Barbara Walters: Iconic Interviewer 8

Katharine Graham: Fighting for a Free Press 10

Anna Wintour: Queen of Fashion 12

Oprah Winfrey: Succeeding through Struggle 14

Shonda Rhimes: The Showrunner 16

Jennifer Salke: Television's Hitmaker 18

Donna Langley: Hollywood Visionary 20

Helen Thomas: First Lady of the Press 22

Katharine Viner: Meeting Today's Challenges 24

Christiane Amanpour: Courageous War Reporter 26

Out of the Shadows 28

Glossary 30

Read More 31

Index 32

About the Author 32

1

Gwen Ifill: Television Pioneer

Growing up, Gwen Ifill watched the news every night. None of the news anchors looked like her. In 2013, things came full circle. She became the first African American woman to co-anchor a network broadcast.

Gwendolyn Ifill was born in New York City in 1955. Both of her parents were Caribbean immigrants. Ifill and her siblings read the daily paper. Her parents encouraged discussion of the day's events at dinner. When Ifill was nine years old, she already knew she wanted to be a journalist.

Ifill graduated from Simmons College in 1977. She was hired as a food writer at the *Boston Herald-American* that year. In 1981, she started covering politics for the *Baltimore Evening Sun*. She went on to cover politics in the *Washington Post* and the *New York Times*.

Gwen Ifill on set of *PBS NewsHour* in 2012.

In 1994, Ifill began her career in television journalism. She was the Capitol Hill reporter for NBC. Five years later, she became the moderator of PBS's *Washington Week in Review*. In 2013, her reputation for fairness helped her get the co-anchor position on *PBS NewsHour*.

Ifill with vice presidential nominee Senator Joe Biden at the 2008 debate.

Ifill believed it was important to have diverse voices in journalism. She mentored many young girls and people of color. In 2016, at age 61, Ifill died of cancer.

THINK ABOUT IT

Many journalists believe in objectivity. They try not to let their opinions or life experiences affect their work. But Ifill said she didn't believe in objectivity. She believed in fairness. What do you think she meant?

20
Number of questions Gwen Ifill asked at the 2004 vice-presidential debate

- She moderated two vice-presidential debates, in 2004 and 2008.
- In 2004, she asked what should be done to treat the high rate of AIDS among African American women. Neither candidate knew what to say.
- Ifill moderated the 2008 debate with a broken ankle.

Samantha Bee: Commenting with Comedy

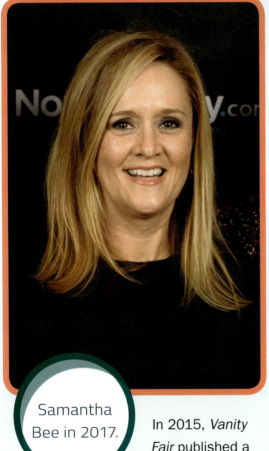

Samantha Bee in 2017.

out of her eyes. This mix of humor and anger is what Bee does well.

Bee was born in Ontario, Canada, in 1969. She moved between her divorced parents' homes and her grandmother's house. She was a rebellious teenager. But she did well in school. A college theater class introduced her to acting.

Bee was in several comedy groups in the 1990s. She cofounded an all-female comedy group called the Atomic Fireballs. In 2003, she became the first female correspondent on *The Daily Show*. She spent 12 years there.

In 2015, *Vanity Fair* published a photo of several late-night TV hosts. They were all men. In response, Samantha Bee photoshopped herself into the picture—as a centaur, with lasers shooting

In 2015, Bee was offered her own show. *Full Frontal with Samantha Bee* started airing in 2016. It became the No. 1 show for people aged 18–34. In 2017, Bee was on *Time* magazine's list of the 100 most influential people.

310,000
Downloads of Samantha Bee's "This is Not a Game: The Game" mobile app

- The app was released in 2018, ahead of the midterm elections.
- It used comedy and trivia games to educate players on political topics.
- Players earned cash for correct answers and for registering to vote.

SATIRE AND THE NEWS

Satire is a form of humor that mocks or criticizes. Political satire exposes hypocrisy by politicians or governments. It has existed since the fourth century BCE. In modern times, comedians use political satire in news-style programs. *Saturday Night Live*'s "Weekend Update" has been around for over 40 years. Jon Stewart was famous for the political satire he did on *The Daily Show* (1999–2015). Many viewers come to these shows for comedy, but they also learn about politics.

Barbara Walters: Iconic Interviewer

Barbara Walters was born in Boston in 1929. Her father was a nightclub owner. Walters spent a lot of time in her father's nightclubs. She watched stars perform. She saw them take off their makeup backstage. She realized they were ordinary people. This helped her interview celebrities later in life.

Walters graduated from Sarah Lawrence College in 1951. Her first job in TV was as an assistant publicity director. In 1961, she worked as a writer for NBC's *The Today Show*. She eventually wrote, edited, and reported her own stories. Known as "the Today girl," she was not allowed to cover serious topics like politics. These were for men.

In 1976, she cohosted the *ABC Evening News* with Harry Reasoner. He did not like working with a woman. In 1978, Walters left the news to focus on her interview specials. She interviewed hundreds of guests on the investigative news show *20/20*. She stayed on the show until 2004.

In 1997, Walters created and starred in *The View*, a daytime talk show hosted by women. Although she retired from the air in 2014, she still works on the show as executive producer.

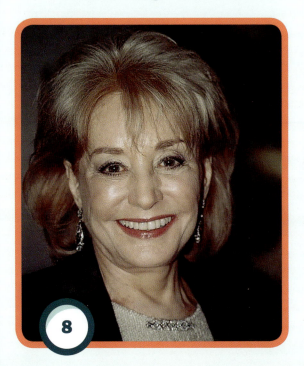

Walters and her cohosts on *The View* interview President Barack Obama in 2010.

THE WALTERS INTERVIEW

Walters created a style of interviewing all her own. She would go to the homes of celebrities and politicians. Viewers felt they were watching a conversation between friends. She mixed hard journalism with understanding. Many famous people, including Oprah Winfrey, cried during their interviews. Others revealed parts of their personalities people hadn't seen before.

$1 million
Annual salary Walters received when she joined ABC in 1976

- Walters earned $500,000 for co-anchoring the *ABC Evening News* and $500,000 for hosting interview specials.
- This made her the highest-paid journalist of her time, angering many male journalists.
- Newspapers called her the "million-dollar baby."

4

Katharine Graham: Fighting for a Free Press

Katharine Graham in 1975.

For most of her life, Katharine Graham was shy and insecure. Then, at 46, she became the president of the *Washington Post*. Graham found her inner strength. She championed the freedom of the press.

Katharine Meyer was born in New York City in 1917. Her father was a self-made millionaire. He bought the *Post* in 1933.

Graham was close to her father. After graduating college, she went to Washington, DC, to write for the paper.

In 1940, she married Philip Graham. Her father gave him ownership of the paper. Katharine stayed home with their four children. Philip struggled with manic depression. He committed suicide in 1963. Katharine became head of the paper. She learned about the company. She realized things could be done better.

In 1965, Graham hired Ben Bradlee to run the *Post*. The paper became known for its investigative journalism. In 1971, they gained access to the Pentagon Papers. These documents showed that the US Government had lied about the Vietnam War. The *New York Times* had been sued for publishing parts of these documents. Graham's lawyers warned her not to publish. She decided to do it anyway.

Graham's support for a free press was tested again in 1972. There had been a break-in at the Watergate hotel. Journalists at the *Post* had proof that President Richard Nixon was involved. Nixon said the paper was lying. But the *Post*'s source was accurate. Nixon was forced to resign.

6
Number of years it took Katharine Graham to write her autobiography

- *Personal History* won a Pulitzer Prize in 1998.
- Graham originally wanted to call it *Two Lives*. Journalist Nora Ephron said it represented Graham's journey through four lives—as daughter, wife, widow, and woman.
- The movie *The Post* (2017), starring Meryl Streep, is based on Graham's book.

Graham with the *Post* in 1964.

Anna Wintour: Queen of Fashion

Anna Wintour is known as the most powerful person in fashion. She was born in London in 1949. Her father was a famous newspaper editor. He told her when she was young that she would one day be the editor of *Vogue* magazine.

At 15, Wintour cut her hair into the bob style she's known for. At 16, she dropped out of school to enjoy the nightlife of 1960s London. In 1976, she moved to New York City. She started working at *Harper's Bazaar* as a fashion editor. She held similar positions at other magazines.

In 1988, Wintour came to *Vogue* as editor-in-chief. She quickly made changes. The first magazine cover under her leadership mixed affordable and expensive clothing. She was the first in the industry to put celebrities on the cover. These changes led to huge sales and advertising partnerships.

Wintour's success at the magazine made her a superstar. She has supported some of the most recognizable names

Anna Wintour in 2019.

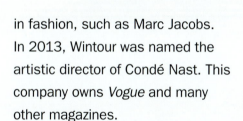

Former First Lady Michelle Obama joins Anna Wintour for her grand opening in 2014.

in fashion, such as Marc Jacobs. In 2013, Wintour was named the artistic director of Condé Nast. This company owns *Vogue* and many other magazines.

VOGUE AND BODY IMAGE

Models in *Vogue* are much thinner than the average person. Some of them have eating disorders and other health problems. Readers, including girls and young women, compare their own bodies to the models. This causes body image issues. In 2012, *Vogue* promised to start using models that help promote a healthy body image.

$30,000
Cost of a ticket to the 2018 Met Gala

- Anna Wintour has run this glamorous event since 1999. It is held each year to raise money for the Metropolitan Museum of Art's Costume Institute.
- The Gala brings together celebrities like Beyoncé, Nick Jonas, Rihanna, and Michael B. Jordan with top fashion designers.
- In 2014, the Met renamed its costume institute the Anna Wintour Costume Center.

6

Oprah Winfrey: Succeeding through Struggle

She was born poor in Kosciusko, Mississippi, in 1954. Her birth name was "Orpah," after a biblical character. But Oprah was easier to pronounce. She lived with her grandmother until she was seven. She learned to read at three. Books became a comfort and an escape.

The rest of Winfrey's childhood was a struggle. She moved between her parents' homes. She was sexually abused. At 14, she became pregnant. The baby died soon after birth. Even with these challenges, Winfrey earned a scholarship to Tennessee State University.

She graduated from college in 1976. She became the co-anchor of a TV news program in Baltimore. A TV executive saw her and invited her to host *A.M. Chicago*. This became the *Oprah Winfrey Show*. It ran for 25 years and was the highest-rated talk show in history. Winfrey's emotionally honest approach attracted millions of viewers.

In 1996, Winfrey started Oprah's Book Club. The books she selected became best sellers. Products featured on her Oprah's Favorite Things episodes

Oprah Winfrey in 2017.

Winfrey addresses school violence on her show in 1988.

290
Number of girls per year who attend Oprah Winfrey's Leadership Academy for Girls (OWLAG) in South Africa

- Winfrey started the school in 2007 after a conversation with former South African President Nelson Mandela.
- Each year, over 6,000 girls apply to the school.
- Winfrey considers the students her children. They call her "Mom O."

THINK ABOUT IT
It is said that Winfrey is the same person on TV as she is off TV. Would this be hard to do? Do you think this has contributed to her success? Explain your answer.

would fly off the shelves. Her mass influence became known as the Oprah Effect.

Winfrey also has her own production company, Harpo Productions, Inc. In 2000, she started *O, The Oprah Magazine*. In 2011, she launched her cable channel, the Oprah Winfrey Network (OWN).

7

Shonda Rhimes: The Showrunner

First, she wanted to be a novelist. But that didn't pay well. She decided to try screenwriting. She went to the University of Southern California's School of Cinematic Arts. Her big break came when HBO hired her to write the 1999 movie *Introducing Dorothy Dandridge*.

Shonda Rhimes's influence in TV helped her become a media mogul. She was born in Chicago in 1970. Her parents were intellectuals. They encouraged her to read. She was a natural storyteller. At age four, she tape-recorded stories for her mother to type up. She knew she wanted to be a writer.

Rhimes graduated from Dartmouth College in 1991.

Shonda Rhimes in 2015 (left). And celebrating 300 episodes with the cast of *Grey's Anatomy*.

Rhimes realized that TV was better than books for the characters she wanted to create. The second TV pilot she

made was *Grey's Anatomy*. The series premiered in 2005 on ABC. Tens of millions of viewers tuned in. Rhimes was celebrated for her diverse characters. That year, she also created her own production company, Shondaland.

Rhimes's second show for ABC debuted in 2012. *Scandal* was the first show in almost 40 years to feature an African American woman in a leading role. Like *Grey's Anatomy*, the show was a success with both viewers and critics. Shondaland shows used social media in new ways. Viewers could live tweet with the shows' stars as the episodes aired. Podcasts highlighted behind-the-scenes facts.

In 2015, Rhimes released an inspirational memoir. In it, she detailed an entire year when she said yes to everything. Her "Year of Yes" improved her life and the lives of her three daughters.

8
Number of projects Shonda Rhimes is working on for Netflix

- Rhimes signed the $150-million deal in August 2017.
- She will write for at least two of the projects and produce the rest.
- One new series will be based on the life of New York fashionista and con artist Anna Delvey.

Rhimes speaks at a TED Conference in 2016.

8

Jennifer Salke: Television's Hitmaker

Jennifer Salke is a TV executive with a talent for discovering hit shows. She was born in 1965 and grew up in Los Angeles. While studying at New York University, she met director Martin Scorsese. She spent nine months working with him.

In the early 1990s, Salke worked on the popular shows *Beverly Hills, 90210* and *Melrose Place*. In 2002, she became the senior vice

Jennifer Salke in 2017.

$600,000+
Amount of money raised at a 2019 Operation Smile event co-chaired by Jennifer Salke

- Operation Smile provides life-changing surgery to children in poor countries with cleft facial conditions.
- Every three minutes, a baby is born with a cleft.
- Salke's son was born with a cleft lip. Since 2009, she and her family have worked with Operation Smile.

president of drama development at 20th Century Fox. She spent nine years there. She was responsible for the popular shows *Glee* and *New Girl*.

When Salke joined NBC in 2011, they were fourth in the Nielsen ratings. Under her leadership, they jumped to first place. The biggest

Salke at the world premier of *Jonas Brothers Chasing Happiness* in 2019.

show she bought was *This Is Us*. Salke believed in the drama when her colleagues didn't. It became the network's No. 1 new show.

In 2018, Salke was named the head of Amazon Studios. In a short time, she signed top talent including directors Jordan Peele, who made the hit movie *Get Out*, and Oscar winner Barry Jenkins.

NIELSEN RATINGS

Each year, the Nielsen Company chooses about 40,000 households. There are around 100,000 people in these households. Computers are connected to their TVs. Nielsen tracks the shows they watch. The computers tally which shows are popular and which are not. Advertisers and TV executives depend on Nielsen ratings to decide where to spend money. Shows with bad Nielsen ratings are often canceled.

9

Donna Langley: Hollywood Visionary

Donna Langley in 2016.

Donna Langley is one of the only women to head a major film studio. She was born in 1968. Her biological mother was English. Her biological father was Egyptian. She was adopted by an English family. She has said that being adopted gave her a sense of independence.

Langley graduated from Kent College. In 1991, she moved to Los Angeles. She found a job as a hostess at a restaurant. It was there that she met film executive Michael De Luca. He invited her to come to work for his company, New Line Cinema. She worked her way up to junior executive. She discovered a film many others had rejected. *Austin Powers* (1997) became a huge success for New Line Cinema.

In 2001, Langley joined Universal Pictures as a senior vice president. She continued to find box-office hits. She started building franchises. These include the *Fast & Furious*

4
Percent of top 100 studio films directed by women from 2007–2018

- Because of this, TIME'S UP and the Annenberg Inclusion Initiative launched the 4% Challenge in 2019.
- The goal is to get film studios to hire more female directors.
- Universal was the first major studio to sign the challenge.

series, the *Despicable Me* series, and *Jurassic Park*. In 2017, Universal made over $5 billion worldwide. This was the most it had ever made in a year.

Langley is also known for funding films with diverse talent and stories. *Straight Out of Compton* (2015) and *Get Out* (2017) both feature African Americans. They address racism. Both were hugely successful for Universal. Langley was named Chairman of Universal Filmed Entertainment Group in 2019.

10

Helen Thomas: First Lady of the Press

Helen Thomas in 2013.

Helen Thomas was not afraid to ask tough questions and challenge authority. She was born in Kentucky in 1920 and grew up in Detroit, Michigan. Her parents were immigrants from modern-day Lebanon. When she saw her name in her high school newspaper, she knew she wanted to be a journalist.

Thomas graduated from Wayne State University in 1942. She moved to Washington, DC. She joined United Press International (UPI) in 1943. She reported on the US Department of Justice and other government agencies.

In 1960, Thomas covered the White House. She achieved many firsts for female journalists. In 1974, she became the first female White House bureau chief for a wire service. At presidential news conferences, she asked the first question. She ended each event by saying, "Thank you, Mr. President."

Thomas was known for asking tough questions. She asked President George W. Bush about the Iraq War in 2006. She questioned President Richard Nixon about Watergate in 1974. She would keep asking her question until she got an answer.

Thomas was respected for being a watchdog over the government, as shown at this press conference in 1981.

10
Number of US presidents Thomas covered in her 68-year career

- She enjoyed covering President John F. Kennedy the most. President George W. Bush was her least favorite president to cover.
- On August 4, 2009, President Barack Obama brought her cupcakes to celebrate their shared birthday.
- Thomas said that every president tried to influence the press in some way.

GOVERNMENT WATCHDOGS

The founders of the US Constitution understood the importance of a free press. The press is considered the fourth branch of the government. The first three branches are the presidential, the judicial, and congress. As the fourth branch, the press provides a check on the power of the other three branches. Journalists are watchdogs over the government.

11

Katharine Viner: Meeting Today's Challenges

Katharine Viner was born in Yorkshire, England, in 1971. At 21, she won a contest to edit the *Guardian* for two weeks. This is one of England's most popular newspapers. From then on, she knew she wanted to be a journalist. She returned to the *Guardian* in 1997.

Viner worked her way up to deputy editor in 2008. In 2013, she led the new *Guardian Australia*. In less than a year, this online-only paper had over 5 million views per month. In 2014, Viner became editor-in-chief of *Guardian US*. This is the paper's online presence in the United States. In 2015, she was named editor-in-chief of Guardian News and Media.

Viner is the company's first female editor-in-chief. When she started her new job, the *Guardian* had been losing money for years. Viner is helping to turn it around. Many newspapers today are shutting down. Others are putting up paywalls so people can't read them online for free. But the *Guardian* is making money, and its content is still free. It has readers all over the world. Many are supporting the paper with financial contributions. These contributions are used to pay for more journalism.

Katharine Viner in 2017.

20+
Number of years in a row the *Guardian* lost money

- The financial year 2018–2019 was the first time since 1998 that the *Guardian* made money.
- Most of its money comes from digital advertising and digital subscriptions.
- Subscriptions are voluntary. Readers don't have to pay. But many choose to pay. They want to support the *Guardian*.

NEWS ON SOCIAL MEDIA

Most Americans get their news from social media. News on these sites isn't always accurate. In 2016, the Russian government posted false stories on Facebook. These stories were labeled as news. Russia posted them to influence the US presidential elections. On social media, phony stories can look like real news.

Christiane Amanpour: Courageous War Reporter

News anchor and war reporter Christiane Amanpour has received every major award in television journalism. She was born in London in 1958. Her mother was British and her father was Iranian. She spent her first 11 years in Iran. Then she was sent to boarding school in England.

Amanpour watched the Iranian Revolution on TV in England. This was in 1979. The ruler of Iran was overthrown. Many people were killed. Amanpour's parents fled the country. Seeing the footage made Amanpour want to be a journalist.

She graduated from the University of Rhode Island in 1983. That year, she got a job at the news station CNN. Amanpour volunteered to go to the most dangerous countries. In 1992, she covered the Bosnian War in Eastern Europe. Bombs and gunfire exploded all around her. The Serbian army was killing civilians. Amanpour was criticized for calling the war a genocide of Muslims. The international community would later agree with her.

Christiane Amanpour in 2015.

Amanpour on assignment in 2012.

As a news anchor, Amanpour interviewed world leaders. She worked for CBS's *60 Minutes* while continuing her field work for CNN. Throughout the early 2000s, she produced several CNN documentaries. She also worked as a news anchor for PBS and ABC. In 2018, she started the hour-long interview program *Amanpour & Company*.

54
Number of journalists worldwide who were killed in 2018

- Some died because they were on dangerous assignments. Some were murdered for being journalists.
- Christiane Amanpour is a senior advisor for the Committee to Protect Journalists (CPJ).
- CPJ works to defend journalists and fights for the freedom of the press.

THINK ABOUT IT

Amanpour risked her life to report in countries during wartime. Do you think getting news footage and telling stories is worth the risk? Why or why not?

Out of the Shadows

Alice Allison Dunnigan

Born in 1906, Dunnigan was a Kentucky schoolteacher. But she wanted to be a journalist. At 13, she wrote one-sentence news items for her local paper. She wrote for newspapers whenever she could. By 1947, she was head of the Associated Negro Press Washington Bureau. She was the first African American woman to cover the White House.

Alice Allison Dunnigan.

Martha Gellhorn

Gellhorn covered almost every major war in the 20th century. Born in 1908, she started as a journalist during the Great Depression (1929–1939). She became friends with First Lady Eleanor Roosevelt. In 1940, she married novelist Ernest Hemingway. When he did not approve of her travels, she left. In 1944, she was the only reporter on the beaches during the D-Day landings.

Marlene Sanders

In 1964, Sanders became the first woman to anchor a nightly newscast. Born in 1931, she went to New York to become an actress. She took an assistant position at a news station. She moved from writer to producer to correspondent. In 1966, she became the first woman to report from Vietnam during the war. She won three Emmy awards.

Ida B. Wells-Barnett

Wells-Barnett was born enslaved in Mississippi in 1862. She became a teacher. When the Civil War ended, African Americans were still being killed. Wells-Barnett became a journalist to expose this racism. She pioneered investigative techniques used in journalism today. She bought part of a newspaper. Her articles were reprinted in over 200 black publications across the United States.

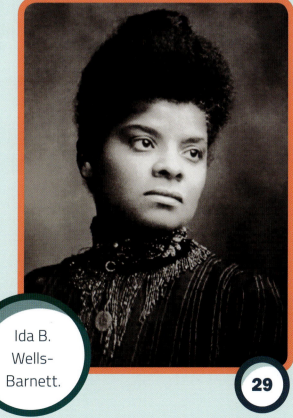

Ida B. Wells-Barnett.

Glossary

anchors
People who read the news on TV.

body image
How someone views and thinks about their body.

correspondent
A journalist who reports news from a distant location.

franchise
A collection of stories that include the same characters and/or the same universe.

freedom of the press
The right to publish information, thoughts, and opinions without restraint or censorship. This right is guaranteed by the First Amendment of the US Constitution.

genocide
An attempt to kill all people from a certain racial, political, religious, or cultural group.

hypocrisy
When someone's actions are different from what they say or what they believe.

journalist
Someone who collects, writes, and/or edits news stories.

mogul
An important person.

pilot
The first episode of a TV show. It is used to try to sell the show to TV networks.

source
A person who shares their knowledge or experiences with journalists. Journalists protect their sources. A document can also be a source.

wire service
A news agency that sends out news by wire or satellite to newspapers, magazines, or TV stations.

Read More

Dell, Pamela. *Understanding the News*. Cracking the Media Literacy Code. North Mankato, MN: Capstone Press. 2019.

Hollihan, Kerrie Logan. *Reporting Under Fire: 16 Daring Women War Correspondents and Photojournalists*. Women of Action. Chicago, IL: Chicago Review Press, 2014.

Mahoney, Ellen. *Nellie Bly and Investigative Journalism for Kids: Mighty Muckrakers from the Golden Age to Today, with 21 Activities*. Chicago, IL: Chicago Review Press, 2015.

Moss, Caroline. *Run the Show Like CEO Oprah Winfrey*. Work It, Girl. Minneapolis, MN: Frances Lincoln Children's Books, 2019.

Rice, Dona Herweck. *Deception: Real or Fake News?*. Huntington Beach, CA: Teacher Created Materials, 2018.

Visit 12StoryLibrary.com

Scan the code or use your school's login at **12StoryLibrary.com** for recent updates about this topic and a full digital version of this book. Enjoy free access to:

- Digital ebook
- Breaking news updates
- Live content feeds
- Videos, interactive maps, and graphics
- Additional web resources

Note to educators: Visit 12StoryLibrary.com/register to sign up for free premium website access. Enjoy live content plus a full digital version of every 12-Story Library book you own for every student at your school.

Index

Amanpour, Christiane, 26-27

Bee, Samantha, 6-7

CNN, 26-27
comedian, 6-7

editors, 12-13, 24-25

film executive, 20-21

Guardian, 24-25
Grey's Anatomy, 16-17
Graham, Katharine, 10-11

Ifill, Gwen, 4-5

journalists, 4-5, 8-9, 22-23, 24-25, 26-27, 28-29, 30

Langley, Donna, 20-21

PBS, 4-5, 27

Rhimes, Shonda, 16-17

Salke, Jennifer, 18-19
screenwriter, 16-17

talk show hosts, 8-9, 14-15
The View, 8-9
Thomas, Helen, 22-23
TV executive, 18-19

Viner, Katharine, 24-25
Vogue, 12-13

Walters, Barbara, 8-9
Washington Post, 10-11
Winfrey, Oprah, 14-15
Wintour, Anna, 12-13

About the Author
Brianna L. DeVore has a bachelor's degree in women's studies and works in the publishing industry. She lives in Minnesota with her husband, cat, and two dogs.

READ MORE FROM 12-STORY LIBRARY

Every 12-Story Library Book is available in many fomats. For more information, visit **12StoryLibrary.com**